A BETTER YEAR AHEAD?

Opening Our Eyes to Hope

Also by Mel Lawrenz—

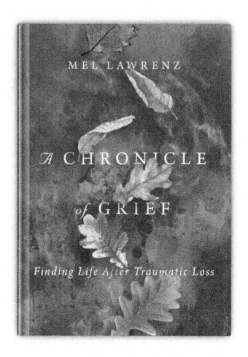

A Chronicle of Grief: Finding Life After Traumatic Loss (IVP, 2020)

In this narrative of grief, Pastor Mel Lawrenz chronicles how his family struggled to survive the sudden death of their beloved daughter. In raw, vivid episodes, he describes the immediacy of the pain and the uncertainty of what comes next. In the agony of loss, Lawrenz apprehends the realities of love and life and offers insights on how any of us can arrange our life priorities before tragedy hits.

"*A Chronicle of Grief* deserves to stand alongside C. S. Lewis's *A Grief Observed*, Gerald Sittser's *A Grace Disguised*, and Nicholas Wolterstorff's *Lament for a Son* as an experience of rawest sorrow transmuted into a testament of deepest hope."

Mark Buchanan, author and professor

Reader Reviews...

"Full of insight and hope... those I gave the book to were deeply comforted."

"Beautifully and eloquently written, this is a book to get and a book to give."

"I have gone through many losses... I came away with renewed hope and encouragement."

"No platitudes, just hard-won wisdom and truth."

"Deeply moving, providing the reader with a path through their grief and sorrow."

"Searingly honest while offering hope for a life beyond loss."

Also by Mel Lawrenz—

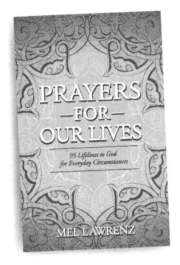

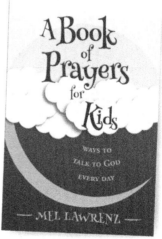

In *Prayers for Our Lives: 95 Lifelines to God for Everyday Circumstances* Mel Lawrenz offers 95 different prayers to be used in times of distress, on special occasions, and as daily patterns. For instance: Morning Prayers • Evening Prayers • Mealtime Prayers • For the Family • For Worship • When We Are Ill • When We Are Discouraged • For Faith and Salvation • When We Are Tempted • For Friends • For the Nation • When Someone Gets Married • Praise to Christ the Lord • Thanks for a Major Achievement • When We Need Guidance • and dozens more.

A Book of Prayers for Kids: Ways to Talk to God Every Day offers dozens of prayers for kids to use for every day, difficult days, and special days.

Reader Reviews...

"My kids love this book!"

"My daughter was having bad dreams often and also experiencing anxiety about certain things. I bought this book and she begin to read the bed time prayer every night, which gave her a since of peace and calmed her anxiety."

"Our four sons aged 4 to 12 have truly enjoyed this book. We read it every night after dinner, before bed. The prayers are so fitting to their lives and the daily issues they face. My 4-year-old loves to recite the prayers over and over. I am so thankful we found this and have been working it into our everyday lives!"

"This book is helping my child speak out her own prayers more confidently."

"Great prayer book, easy to read. Beautiful array of prayers. My son reads 1-2 prayers every night after praying his own prayer."

"This is a beautiful book of prayers. A great gift for grandchildren."

A BETTER YEAR AHEAD?

Opening Our Eyes to Hope

MEL LAWRENZ

WWW.WORDWAY.ORG

Edited by Danae Templeton
Cover and interior design by Sheila Hahn

CONTENTS

Prayers

INTRODUCTION

2020 was a difficult year. Could 2021 be better?

Yes, of course. But what will it take?

There are some things in life we can control, and others we cannot. No one has a magic wand to wave to make things better, and no one has a crystal ball which reveals exactly what we will face in the months and years to come.

But things can be better. Moving into better days ahead means learning how to accept what we cannot change and becoming wiser about what we do influence, all the while looking to God for strength and guidance and perseverance.

This book is a collection of writings and prayers and Scriptures that are about values and choices. Our best chance at better days ahead is by using wisdom and discernment, deciding what we believe and whom we should trust, understanding good and evil, committing to prayer and the reading of Scripture, dealing with loss and depression and doubt, and much more.

The people I admire for their courage in facing the future have both deep faith and real humility. Modesty is stronger than bravado. The way they face their losses is not by denying them, but by mourning them, and then moving forward one step at a time.

Most readings here are published for the first time, and a few come from previously published works. Most of the topics are about personal spiritual matters, not so much the expansive social and political issues of the day which are beyond the scope of this small book.

I don't know about you, but I find myself needing to take time these days to stop and try to figure out just exactly what is happening around us. It is so complex, and so stark. Gaining even a little more clarity will help us have a better year ahead, especially if we discuss the issues with each other.

Mel Lawrenz

More resources, including a discussion guide, at...

www.WordWay.org

A BETTER YEAR AHEAD?

A BETTER YEAR AHEAD?

1

SIZING UP A DIFFICULT YEAR

Everyone I know agrees with this simple sentiment: 2020 was a difficult year. A shockingly difficult year. An unprecedented difficult year. And they all wonder: *Is there reason to hope that the new year might be better?*

Of course, any of us may have that sentiment whenever we've had a difficult year. Loss of a job, a marriage that broke apart, an unwelcome medical diagnosis, a recession, an unexpected bereavement—there are so many ways any of us can have "a bad year." Then we come to the end of December, cross into January, and wonder: *Is it possible for next year to be better than the past one?*

But 2020 was different. Once in a great while, there is a year that goes beyond the normal cycle of gains and losses we all go through. Only once in a very great while there is a year when one's whole country, and (amazingly) the whole world, is shaken in such a way that our faith is tested, our love is strained, and our hope is stretched to its limits.

Of course, the pandemic of COVID-19 is the major precipitating event that made 2020 so difficult, but it was not the only crisis. No matter what you think about the realities of this virus and disease, there is no disputing this: the first pandemic of the 21st century has affected the whole world in one way or another. It has upended our lives, strained our relationships, reshaped our work patterns. This is not the first time the world has been disrupted and confused by a disease, and it will not be the last.

There were other troubles that hit massive numbers of people in 2020. Unprecedented numbers of workers lost their jobs. Racial tensions flared up, revealing the ongoing need for serious social reform. Pockets of radical groups clashed with each other in city streets. We witnessed both peaceful protests and flareups of rage and violence. Opportunists are never far away.

These are the events that dominate the headlines, but there are other powerful social fissures, not yet fully realized, that will challenge us for years to come. What will happen in families where staying at home has not been a blessing of familial togetherness, but an increase of tensions and even domestic violence? How will social distancing affect our relationships long-term? And what about widespread grief on the other side of loss? Most people have not even begun to grieve what they have lost in 2020. We are still in the middle of the losses. Dealing with it all, psychologically and spiritually, will require honesty and courage.

How will disconnectedness and isolation shape us? What will happen to people who lost their businesses? Will people come back to their churches, or will a significant percentage stay away?

And so, we may wonder: *Is there a better year ahead?* The only honest answer is that it depends. We will have to cope with stresses and losses that are beyond our control, but we can indeed have a better year if we make good and wise decisions with what we *can* control. Some of our losses in 2020 were imposed on us, and some, we brought on ourselves.

We can have hope, but not if hope is merely wishful thinking. Hope always leads to a call to action. It is not passive sentiment—it is a powerful engine propelling us toward better days, if we so choose.

Loss does not need to have the final word. On the other side of loss is the possibility of gain. The pandemic of 2020 and beyond has forced companies to redefine productivity. It has forced churches to see themselves as something much more than a series of gatherings. Families have invented new ways to hold together.

Seeing the positive is not to live in denial and put a happy face on loss. That never works, and may set us up for a bigger downfall later. This is a time for us to be ruthlessly honest about the losses we have experienced, at the same time that we hold the door open for better days ahead. If 2020 was horrible for you, admit it. Don't underplay it and don't exaggerate it. If 2020 was not difficult for you, admit that. Lots of people were not negatively affected in 2020. Working from home was just fine. They did not get sick. They held onto their jobs, and their investment accounts may have seen handsome growth.

Self-awareness and other-awareness have never been more important. Some people need to grieve their losses, and others (who have not lost much) need to have more empathy than ever for their neighbors who are bleeding. We need fine-tuned sensibilities now, not simplistic social dogmas. We need to look deeply into the social, spiritual, and psychological undercurrents this past tumultuous year has produced. We need to share in the sufferings of others, and then look for healing. And we need truth.

Is it possible that there is a better year ahead?

Yes, of course. Despite the fact that the Coronavirus will continue to spread for some time to come and our lifestyles will be different from what we were used to, it is always possible for the days ahead to be better. Hope is not the belief that all our problems will go away, but that we will be able to survive and build new strength if our minds perceive reality and our hearts demand what is good.

PRAYER

When Someone is Ill

Dear God,

I am watching someone I love suffer in illness. This is so hard for me to witness. I wish I could do something to take the pain and distress away. I feel so helpless.

I'm not sure what to say and what not to say, so I need your guidance and wisdom. Help me to remain faithful and patient. Help me to think more of _____ than myself. Remove from me any hint of resentment I may have.

Please reach into this situation with your restorative touch. Work in the hidden parts of the body. Help everyone to find connections with good physicians and other health care professionals. Please let _____ have a sense of you as the Great Physician.

Please, dear God, bring to _____ a sense of your loving presence. Help loved ones to know that, too.

We know we do not know the future, but I pray that you help us to see that you hold the future.

Thank you, Lord Jesus, for suffering on our behalf. We need you, great Shepherd of the sheep, to lead us all through the valley of illness.

In Christ's Name, Amen.

(from *Prayers for Our Lives: 95 Lifelines to God for Everyday Circumstances* by Mel Lawrenz)

2

TURNING THE CALENDAR

For most people, turning the calendar from one year to the next prompts a longing for life to go well or be better than the previous year. Some people make New Year's resolutions, which may last a year, a month, or maybe a week or two. Some people just don't bother hoping for something better.

The name "January" comes from the Roman god Janus, the god of gates and doorways—the god of beginnings. He is depicted with two faces, one looking back, the other looking forward.

It would be good if we could move into a new year with something more than a vague wish that things will be better. Some people choose fatalism, but that is not the only option.

In Scripture, we are introduced to a God who doesn't just mark the passing of time, but stands above and apart from time. A caretaker and Lord of the future. The Creator who cares about what he created. This makes perfect sense, of course. What artist would create a masterpiece and not care what happened to it?

This is the idea of *providence*: the belief that God is Creator and stays connected with the creation, both knowing the future and being the caretaker and Lord of it.

Providence is the ongoing activity of God in preserving and governing everything that God has made in the creation. It is exactly what you would expect of a Creator whose work of creating is an act of love. Providence is both care that *precedes* and care that *proceeds*. It is the benevolent attitude of God toward what he has created. God began a great work in creation, and he continues that work.

Naturally, this raises the question of how we can trust in the love and care of God, since we see so much pain and distress in the world. This is an understandable question, which we'll come to a bit later in this book.

One day, a man came to see me who was interested in belief in God but had all the typical major questions. He asked me: How can God keep bringing more people into the world, knowing that there is so much suffering? I had a picture of my two young kids on my bookshelf behind him, and I pointed toward the picture. I told him that my wife and I had experienced suffering and loss as we grew up, and we had a realistic view of life. Yet, we wanted to have kids. Why? Did we do something wrong by wanting to have kids? Did we cause suffering? No, that can't possibly be true. It was good to have those two kids because the goodness of life outweighs the hard times that might befall us. Goodness is greater than pain.

Nobody knows what may happen in the coming year, and that is probably a good thing. Any of us can speculate about the challenges and opportunities, pleasures and pains that may lie ahead. We will move into the future. But we cannot live in the future any more than we can live in the past. The present day is where we have power and choice.

Believing in the providence of God means that the future is not a matter of random chance. We can call out to God for comfort and guidance and assurance. We can always ask God how things are meant to be.

More than the idea of a deity with two faces who looks ahead and behind, the biblical God is above all reality, encompassing in his vision and embracing in his power past, present, and future.

God is never surprised by what happens, but is alternately pleased and displeased by it. God points us in the direction of a good future, leading us toward a life goal that no human being would have conceived. We are not the victims of fate. God intended us to be responsible beings, created to be like God, making better and better choices.

The good path is always just the next few steps in the direction of the good end.

3

DEALING WITH LOSS

Having a better year ahead depends on our honest assessment of what we have been through in the past. That includes assessing our blessings and our losses. When we honestly and accurately assess our true losses, we are in a better place to move on to potentially better days.

We need to understand the people in our lives who have gone through significant loss. One of the most purposeful things any of us can do is to show compassion and to be present with those who have suffered loss. We all have different preferred ways of doing that. Whether we prefer sending a card or an email, responding on social media, having a face-to-face conversation, picking up the phone, or sending flowers, that's fine. We just need to do *something.* Don't believe that the best thing is always to give your friend or loved one space.

We cannot ignore loss, and we must not multiply it. I am running into more and more people who have suffered one loss on top of another—within their families, in their jobs, in their churches. Some losses we cannot prevent. But we should avoid creating more loss.

There is nothing generic about grief. Somehow, we have to have empathy. To try to understand. To put ourselves in the shoes of the mourner. At the same time, we have to realize that we will never comprehend what this particular loss means to this particular person. It is a kind of "empathy gap." It's no one's fault. It's just inevitable. But, knowing we have an empathy gap, we can choose to have compassion that goes beyond our comprehension.

Along the way, if it is indeed true that "faith, hope, and love" are "the things that remain" (1 Cor. 13:13), then we rehearse what we really believe (faith), trust that things will be okay (hope), and cherish, cherish, cherish (love) both those within arm's reach and those who have slipped beyond. Love has no end.

We have to look straight at our losses, or else comfort will be truncated. This is not to say we should obsess about our losses. Focusing only on our losses hour after hour, day after day, is a skewing of reality. The real world includes that loss, which is that ugly gaping hole, but it also includes all the things that remain and the people that remain and the qualities that remain like faith, hope, and love. When we obsess about our losses, we give them more power than they should have. We are going to have to live in a new reality that includes the loss but also good meals, normal conversations with people about the normal things of life, good stories in books or movies. Life goes on. Even in our losses, we have to lean into the good, otherwise we contradict the good blessings we enjoyed.

A few weeks after my wife and I lost our 30-year-old daughter, I found myself getting caught up in all life's normal responsibilities and concerns and forgetting in the middle of the day what had happened to us. Usually, this happened in the early afternoon. When reality hit, when I remembered, the pain was like a knife thrust into my gut. This happened every day. I decided that I needed to keep the loss in a part of my mind in my peripheral vision. This is hard to describe. It was like holding something in your hand, your arm stretched out and to the side. I wanted to remember the loss, because then it wouldn't slip into a hidden place and come jumping out at me. I couldn't keep hearing the news in my head as if it were happening again and again.

No wonder grief is draining.

I have known many people over the years who have lost one of their kids. But only after our loss did I know that I had no idea what their pain was like. I was trying to be empathetic. When I did funerals for young people, I tried so hard to comprehend their devastation. But I could not fully understand until it happened to us.

That leaves us with a dilemma. When a friend goes through the worst, whatever that is for them, we are never going to be able to fully understand if it is not something we have been through. When a friend is plunged into the worst, we can—and should—try to imagine what it would be like if the same happened to us. But we are just not able to fully comprehend it if we ourselves have not experienced that particular kind of loss.

So, what do we do? Obviously, it would be wrong to not even try to empathize. But we know we can't honestly say, "I understand," if we have not walked that same path.

What we can and must do is spend a little mental and emotional energy to try to comprehend the friend's loss, remembering that we cannot fully understand, that there is an empathy gap. It is no one's fault. There is no way to close the gap. We have to acknowledge the gap and try to extend our love out over it.

So, we shouldn't say, "I understand," if we have not been through the same thing. We might say "I have no words," or "I can't imagine," or "I'm so, so sorry," or "I am here. I am thinking of you today." That is honest, and it is helpful.

If we can do that for others, we are not filling the hole but standing around it with them, showing that while something or someone good is gone, not everything is gone.

(adapted from *A Chronicle of Grief: Finding Life After Traumatic Loss* by Mel Lawrenz, IVP 2020, used by permission)

PRAYER

When We Are Discouraged

Lord, I am discouraged today.

I had hoped the problems I am encountering would begin to get resolved a long time ago.

I had hoped I would know exactly what I could do to make things better.

I had hoped that other people would see that they are causing problems.

I had hoped that I could be a better person than I am.

I had hoped I could at least have a glimmer of hope.

I feel like I'm holding on by a thread. Some days it seems like I'm walking on the edge of a cliff. I know this is not good. I know it is not safe.

So today, dear God, I just ask you to help me hang in there. I intend to walk in faith today, but I may need extra help.

You are a God of great goodness. I do thank you for your great acts and your mercies in the past. I know that when all else seems disappointing, and when I am deeply discouraged by the people around me, you remain faithful. Your goodness and greatness will never change.

Help me to hold on to you.

Amen.

(from *Prayers for Our Lives: 95 Lifelines to God for Everyday Circumstances* by Mel Lawrenz)

4

WHAT SHOULD I BELIEVE?

Now *that* is an important question. Everything we do in life, every choice we make, every reaction we have to the people in our lives, every opinion we have about how things are going in our communities and our nation, flow out of that structure hidden deep in our minds and hearts: what we believe.

Some of our beliefs are good perceptions of reality, but some are mistakes. Someone once said (and it has been repeated many times): "It doesn't matter what you believe as long as you are sincere." What utter nonsense. Of course it matters what we believe. Unfounded beliefs can kill us, literally. Belief is about reality, not about feeling or preference. Sincerity of belief is only as good as the soundness of the belief.

My wife and I used to live in a house right where a state highway made a perfect 90 degree turn. Once in a while, in the middle of the night, we heard the screech of tires and a decisive *thump*. Then silence. One more driver who believed the road ahead was straight, but discovered the hard truth that there was a 90 degree turn. It didn't matter that they believed the road was straight. It didn't matter that their belief was sincere. Ditches have a way of asserting themselves.

Reality rules every time.

Once I was in a conversation with a friend about alien life forms and whether it is possible they have visited Earth. Her comment struck me: "I could believe that." That was an honest statement. But, of course, the issue is not what we *could* believe, but what we *should* believe. The issue is whether there is *evidence* to believe something is true. Now that takes some work. We have to think. We have to listen to sources of evidence, and before that, judge the *reliability* of the sources of evidence. Some people don't want to do that work. They just want to know who to follow, nodding in agreement on every issue.

So let's break this down. What are the steps each of us should take in deciding what we should believe? There are specific methods for this. Historically proven steps. This applies to whether you are deciding to accept your doctor's analysis that you have cancer, or what source to turn to for weather forecasts, or whether someone is guilty of a crime. There is a wonderful consistency in the proper steps of seeking truth.

Here is one way of describing that progression.

Step 1. *Ask good questions.*

Oftentimes in life finding answers is not that difficult. The issue is whether we are asking the right questions.

Here are some good questions: *How can I be a better person? Whom do I know who knows what is right and wrong? What does it mean to live a good life? What are my core responsibilities as a parent? What is the law of the land, and how can I be committed to it?*

Here are some inferior questions: *How can I feel good? What's in it for me? How can I avoid people who make me uncomfortable? Why are those other people so despicable? How can I hoard what I have? How can I cheat in order to win? Who has raw power and how can I attach myself to them?*

Our instincts about what questions to ask in life reveal the disposition of our minds and hearts. Before we go looking for answers, we need to ask ourselves whether we are asking good, life-giving questions.

Step 2. *Gather evidence, and judge its reliability.*

Let's say someone tells you that if you put some money in their investment account, you are guaranteed that your money will double in five years. You are attracted to the possibility. But it seems too good to be true. (Most things that seem too good to be true, are not true at all.) You need evidence that this claim is reliable. So you research the financial entity. You find reviews from reliable publications. You call your brother who is a banker and ask his opinion. You ask more questions of the person making the offer, including "What do you mean 'guarantee'?" knowing that there is no such thing with investments. Before going any further, you turn away for lack of reliable evidence.

Step 3. *Keep an open mind.*

For some issues in life there is a range of evidence. Look at any courtroom trial. "Guilty" is one possibility; "not guilty" the opposite. Maybe it only takes a day-long trial to look at the evidence, or maybe a month. Jurors are sworn to keep an open mind. And the jury selection process is supposed to weed out potential jurors who are incapable of keeping an open mind.

A long time ago I was called up for jury duty. It felt weighty and sobering. In the jury selection process before each trial the judge looked at all of us potential jurors and said: "The most important duty of a member of jury is to evaluate the credibility of the witnesses and the evidence." I'll never forget that. It makes perfect sense, of course. And, imperfect as a jury trial can be, it still is one of the best alternatives for discovering the truth of a matter. Sometimes a life or death matter. I have never been accused of a crime and have never been on trial, but if I were, and if I were innocent, I'd want to look over at the faces of the jurors and see concentration, focus, and signs of open-mindedness. I would want the jury to do the work to come to the rational, evidence-based belief of my innocence.

This is why bias kills us. It is prejudice: to pre-judge. I don't want members of a jury to make assumptions about me because of how I look or because I am different from them. I need them to be open-minded. Fair-minded. Unbiased. Objective. Impartial.

We owe this to each other. And we owe it to the truth. True impartiality and fair-mindedness is a great gift.

To be open-minded means that once in a while we will change our minds. We break from the pack. We show some independence of thought. To go along with the gang is weakness. To have independent thought is strength.

Step 4. *Explore different answers.*

Let's say you grew up in a home that was 100% committed to one political party. Let's say this not only meant that your parents always voted along the party line, but they also believed that it was necessary to agree with every point and every sub-point in the party's platform. Even if the platform changed over the years. Even if what you were supposed to believe was one thing ten years ago, and something different today. Party loyalty was an all-or-nothing proposition.

Most people know that, in spite of party loyalty, they may find some points on which they have a very different belief. This should come as no surprise. Policy positions are complicated and diverse and fluid in some ways.

Deciding what you believe means exploring different answers. Many people of faith will say they personally believed one thing about the criminal justice system years ago, but they look at it differently now having gone through the process of asking good questions, gathering evidence, keeping an open mind, and exploring different answers. The same is true for many issues.

When we decide what we believe we are building a foundation on which we can base our lives, all the while being humble enough to change our minds on some of the details as we mature and grow.

Step 5. *Come to a conclusion.*

At some point we conclude what we believe. It may be like a light coming on one day, or it may be like gradually waking up in the morning. On the really big issues of life, like whether we believe that God exists or whether Jesus Christ is the Savior, we don't expect to move in and out of that belief. On other detailed matters we take a position in what we believe while being open-minded to new evidence that may come along at any time. There is no crime in changing one's mind on climate change or economic theory or the denomination of the church you attend. There are some major issues in life that we will only understand after we mature. Or after we have suffered.

Step 6. *Test it in real life.*

All of our beliefs will be tested by real life. When my 30-year-old daughter, whom we loved and cherished from the day she was born, suddenly died, all of my beliefs were challenged. My faith beliefs were not nullified, but they were re-ordered, and that for the good. From that time three and a half years ago, until today, and until the day I die, I know that the providence of God and the goodness of God are two truths I will always cling to. These beliefs helped my wife and son and me get through the terrible loss.

When I realize I have come to believe something I had never thought of before, I know that real life will put it to the test. Sometimes we need to believe something even though it seems to contradict common sense. But that is only an apparent contradiction.

All true beliefs move toward a harmony that builds and builds.

We should never believe things merely because someone is shouting them loudly and relentlessly. We can do better, we must do better, than just belonging to a herd that moves thoughtlessly along.

5

WHY DO BAD THINGS HAPPEN?

One balmy summer evening, a storm system started moving up the horizon until it covered about half the sky. I stood out on the front yard of our house to examine a sky that was like a bed with covers pulled partway up. Heavy, dark clouds were moving fast and low, with towering thunderheads and a bulbous underbelly. Something dramatic was coming.

Then a very bizarre thing happened—before the rain ever started falling, with the sun still shining above, I saw a light object in the sky, tumbling downward. Then another and another. I started gathering the objects along with my son, daughter, and wife, though all us should have been inside the house because of the approaching lightning.

A shredded leaf of corn, a piece of roofing material, a page from a cookbook, a golf scorecard with a label from a country club in Stoughton, Wisconsin—all tumbled from high in the open sky along with bits of torn leaves.

At first it was strange and quite amusing, like a game in which you wonder what the next object will be. But as I grew in awareness that this must be the by-product of a tornado somewhere (what else could it be?), it became a more sober experience. I hoped no one had been killed.

Only half an hour later, television news reported that a tornado had been sighted in Stoughton—some 90 miles away—and that homes and a clubhouse at a golf course had been damaged. Pieces of debris had been carried several miles and sprinkled out ahead of the storm system.

It sent a chill up my spine to think I was holding the pieces of someone else's life. What happened? What will happen for these people?

Why do bad things happen in life? And why does God allow them?

Suffering is the great mystery we all face sooner or later.

When you are face-to-face with somebody who has suddenly lost a loved one, or is going through great physical pain or some other kind of anguish, even if you produce a flawless 500-page answer that fits all the pieces together, that answer will still not replace what that person has lost. The suffering person is still going to say, "Why, oh why, does this have to be?"

In the light of the fact that Scripture does not have God giving a simple cause and effect explanation, neither should we. It is critically important for loving friends to be there and say, "This is not the way things were supposed to be, but we are here with you and God is with you."

Romans 8, which says the whole of creation groans "as in the pains of childbirth," it is "subjected to frustration," and it "waits in eager expectation" for God's final redemption, when the bondage will end and the adoption of sons and daughters of God will be complete (Rom. 8:18-39).

Scientists have been saying for a long time that aggressive viruses can be one of the greatest threats to humanity. This is part of the natural world.

Suffering has become nature's abnormal state. In Genesis 3, it says that the newly cursed world now has enmity and pain and conflict. Even the natural order of things, the way nature itself behaves, has been disrupted because of this moral earthquake.

While there are natural catastrophes like tornadoes, hurricanes, and earthquakes, much suffering in the world has human causes.

We cannot prevent a virus from forming. But human choices will influence how far and wide a pandemic spreads. Some diseases cannot be prevented or treated, and some can.

We experience suffering, in other words, because we are just small parts of a whole creation that has its good days and bad days. Sometimes we forget that we are part of a very complex system of cause and effect. If it rains and ruins your family picnic, or floods one region, that same rain might be what saves a farmer's crops. We will never see or understand all the connections.

I find that sometimes, when suffering hits, we can think of reality like this: here is God, and here am I. If I am suffering, I ask "God, why are you doing this to me?" But if I draw a picture of reality where I am a part of a whole world system—one person in a multitude of human beings along with the mountains and rivers and the land and the seas—then I can say that one of my loved ones contracted a disease because we live in a world where there are a lot of diseases on the loose. Some of them are because we have dumped pollutants and carcinogens into our environment. Some of them are because our bodies are frail and temporary. But when I get sick, it is not God doing it to me.

When we understand that we are each part of a whole complex world, a creation that works beautifully sometimes but sometimes breaks and cracks, we are reminded of our moral duty in this life. Instead of us asking God why he allows poverty and famine and injustice, God could turn to us and ask: *Why are you allowing it? Are you using your energy and resources to work against injustice and poverty? What will you do to alleviate suffering? I am the Savior—but you are my assistants.*

Humans go to war, engage in street violence, abuse substances, put themselves at risk. In a modern world where most places have the means to move food (unless it becomes a political weapon), not even drought has to mean famine.

Many people ask, "Why can't God prevent people from causing suffering?" The answer is that he could, and someday he will. God will decisively interrupt the affairs of the world and judgment will come, along with a new creation in which there are no more tears and no more pain (Rev. 21:4). In the meantime, God allows human beings to exercise one of the most noble and most dangerous qualities we possess: freedom.

Freedom is one of our highest values. On D-Day, men ran up beaches under withering gunfire, laying down their lives to gain the freedom of others.

To be human means to be free. That is the way God made us—it's the way things were meant to be. But the very meaning of freedom is that we are free to choose good or evil. It is the only way freedom works. To be human means to have freedom, whether we use it or abuse it.

Why do bad things happen to innocent people? Frequently, it is because human beings act carelessly, cruelly, and maliciously toward each other. Of course, it leaves us asking: *Why? Why must this be?*

Could God have created humanity without this awesome power to choose? Yes, he could have, but then we would be robots and not human beings. We would not know a single moment of chosen love or devotion or goodness. We would not be able to worship God or love our children or our friends. We would be incapable of understanding grace instead of greed, light instead of darkness.

God wanted to make a certain kind of creature as the last step of the creation. He created human beings with this incredible privilege and power, the life-giving and life-taking power of freedom. The misuse of freedom has set into human nature a series of fault lines that go not only through humanity, but through the whole creation.

6

CAN ANYTHING GOOD COME OUT OF SUFFERING?

Most people who suffer something significant wonder whether there is any purpose in it. Our first responsibility to those who suffer is to show compassion and empathy, but there are answers to the question of redemption in suffering.

It is not that God causes evil and suffering for a good end. That is a cruel notion. The issue is whether there is anything good that can happen on the other side of suffering, or even in the midst of the suffering.

1. Suffering can lead to a renewal of faith (2 Cor. 1:9; 4:7; 11:30; 12:9)

Second Corinthians provides some honest truths about suffering. For instance, Paul says that in his heart he felt under the sentence of death, but his circumstances resulted in not relying on himself but "on God who raises the dead" (2 Cor. 1:9). Suffering has a way of pushing to the margins of life all the issues that are truly marginal. It points out what really matters in life, what will matter 20 years from now and 50 years from now. Suffering can have a purifying effect. Second Corinthians 4:7 says, "we have this treasure in jars of clay to show that this all-surpassing power is from God and not from us." In 11:30, Paul says "if I must boast, I will boast of the things that show my weakness." During days of suffering, Paul was driven to the grace of God. He came to believe that God's grace was sufficient and God's power was made perfect through weakness.

2. Suffering can equip us to help others (2 Cor. 1:4)

When we're going through troubles and experience God's comfort, we come out the other side better able to "comfort those in trouble with the comfort that we ourselves received from God." It is good to be able to be a lifeline to someone suffering as we have. It is good to know you are not alone.

3. Suffering can chasten us in appropriate ways (Heb. 12:4-11)

Hebrews 12 teaches that sometimes, when we suffer because of the poor choices we have made and we live through the consequences, we experience a kind of chastening. There are lessons to be learned through suffering which may lessen our self-imposed suffering in the future.

Are there ways we can get through a time of suffering in life by looking beyond it? Yes.

Many people tell stories of how God helped them in their sufferings in ways totally unexpected.

This is the way of the suffering Savior.

4. Christ is a past pioneer (Isa. 53:3; Heb. 4:15)

Jesus was "despised and rejected, a man of sorrows, and familiar with suffering," but he was not a victim (Isa. 53:3). Hebrews 4:15 says that "we do not have a high priest who is unable to sympathize with our weaknesses."

5. Christ is a present help (Matt. 11:28-30; 12:20; Rom. 8:26-27)

Jesus said, "Come to me all you who are weary and burdened, and I will give you rest. Take my yoke upon you and learn from me, for I am gentle and humble in heart, and you will find rest for your souls." The prophets Isaiah had said "A bruised reed he will not break, and a smoldering wick he will not snuff out,"

6. God gives us a future hope (Rom. 8:18-21; 37-38)

Romans 8, verse 18 says, "I consider that our present sufferings are not worth comparing with the glory that will be revealed in us . . . Neither life nor death, neither angels nor demons, neither the present nor the future, nor any powers, neither height nor depth, will be able to separate us from the love of God that is in Christ Jesus our Lord." When God's Word talks to us about looking past pain, it is not to deny the reality of what we may be experiencing today. Most people who experience natural catastrophes believe things will be okay in the future. What that future might be—they don't know. None of us know.

It is not easy to believe that good things can happen in our lives on the other side of some severe suffering. It may take us a long time to realize that is true. Faith and trust is never forced. But when we stand with each other, no matter what we can comprehend or believe, we are already blessed by walking the difficult path and not being alone.

7

WHEN DEPRESSION SETS IN

"The human spirit can endure in sickness, but a crushed spirit who can bear?" (Prov. 18:14).

Depression is rising in our communities. That's a longtime trend, and the stress and isolation of recent times has led to more and more depression.

But there is hope.

Several years ago, the shocking news of the suicide of actor Robin Williams left millions of people all over the world with a mystery: How could someone known for a whole-face smile that caused multitudes of people to laugh to the point of tears be so distraught and dark that he would take his own life? Many were perplexed, and there were many others who said to themselves: *If anyone knew how desperately depressed I am, they would be surprised.*

I write as someone who has seen depression across numerous generations in my own family, and as a pastor who has officiated at the funerals of those who have taken their own lives.

Many people turn to the Scriptures to understand and, if they look widely, they will find not only the hope the Scriptures offer, but also the honesty and accuracy with which the Scriptures account for one of the most common inner maladies of all time: depression.

King David despaired of life more than once. Not only do we have dozens of "Psalms of Lament," but we have physiological descriptions of the effects of the broken heart, as in Psalm 38: "there is no health in my body. . . . my guilt has overwhelmed me, like a burden too heavy to bear . . . . I am bowed down and brought very low. . . all day long I go about mourning . . . . I am feeble and utterly crushed . . . . my heart pounds, my strength fails me . . . . I am like the deaf, who cannot hear, like the mute, who cannot speak . . . . I am about to fall, and my pain is ever with me . . . . LORD, do not forsake me."

This is not a description of "feeling low," sad, or unhappy, but rather what can happen when sadness deepens into despair and then into a physical condition.

Even powerful and successful people can be brought low in depression. The prophet Elijah defeated the false prophets of Baal on Mount Carmel in a stunning victory by God. And yet, fleeing the wrath of Jezebel, Elijah went into isolation and prayed, "I have had enough, LORD, take my life, I am no better than my ancestors" (1 Kings 19:4-5).

God did not condemn Elijah for being destitute and depressed. God did not say: *Buck up, man. Where is your faith? Shake it off.* Instead, an angel of God came, touched Elijah, and offered fresh-baked bread and a jar of water (1 Kings 19:5-6). This is the way God is. "The LORD is close to the brokenhearted and saves those who are crushed in spirit" (Ps. 34:18).

At a desperate moment, the prophet Jonah wanted to die: "Now, LORD, take away my life, for it is better for me to die than to live" (Jonah 4:3). Yes, that is in the Bible. One of the most significant spiritual leaders in Old Testament history came to the point of wondering if he wanted to live or not.

And then there is Job, whose illnesses and profound losses made him despair of life—his wife and "friends" did not help. In the end, God did not offer Job answers for his questions, but instead, God offered himself.

This is what God does and what we must do for each other—be a caring presence. What makes deep depression dangerous is isolation. Often, someone else needs to help the depressed person get connected with the right medical and spiritual resources. We need to know when we are the right people to make those connections. None of us should be put off if our well-meaning words do nothing to help a depressed friend. That may be the time when we need to do less talking and just be there.

As one desperate man said, "Anyone who withholds kindness from a friend forsakes the fear of the Almighty" (Job 6:14).

If difficult times have pushed you down into serious depression, let someone know. Reach out to your physician. Find trusted, wise confidants (particularly those who know about depression) and connect with a counselor. Far too many people suffer deeply inside, not letting anyone else know. There is nothing to be ashamed or afraid of about letting the right people know where you really are.

And for those of us who know someone who has become deeply depressed, we need to be there for them. There is not one simple thing we can tell them to do to raise them up. If someone has sunk low, it took a while to get there, and it will take a while to heal. We need to be compassionate listeners, to nullify shame, and to support them as they seek the help they need.

PRAYER

When We Are Depressed

Dear God,

I have come to a dark place. This has been developing for a long time. No one understands what is going on in me right now. Even I don't understand it fully.

Why do I have to suffer with this? Why is nothing making me feel any better? Why do I not sense any love or hope?

It is hard for me to remember when I did not feel this way. People tell me there is hope. I want to believe that, but it is difficult. My prayer to you is my call for help. Dear God, help me to know I have not been abandoned.

I am ashamed that I feel this way. I'm embarrassed that I am not able to be the person other people want me to be. But I know that all that matters is who I am in your sight. I know I have your grace and forgiveness. And I admit that I am a sinner, too.

I pray as did David "restore to me the joy of my salvation and grant me a willing spirit, to sustain me." "Let me hear joy and gladness." Let my crushed bones rejoice.

Let me hear the gentle whisper of your voice as did Elijah when he was alone and despondent.

Lord Jesus, you said, "come to me, all you who are weary and burdened, and I will give you rest." That sounds very good.

On this day I make this decision: I rest in you.

Amen.

(from *Prayers for Our Lives: 95 Lifelines to God for Everyday Circumstances* by Mel Lawrenz)

8

THINGS THAT REMAIN: FAITH

Does the word "change" give you a good feeling, or the opposite? For people who have experienced growth and development with little crisis, "change" may have a very positive connotation. But for a person who has experienced loss, "change" automatically sends alert signals. For example, in the workplace when management says, "Change is coming," that very often puts us into a tense and guarded position. Human nature dictates that we wonder: *What might I lose in this "change" equation?*

Life still includes change. Some changes are good, others we have to endure. When a loved one dies. When a kid goes off the rails. When you are laid off. When a pandemic spreads across the world and suddenly your whole life changes.

In 1 Corinthians 13, the Apostle Paul talks about three things that endure and do not change: faith, hope, and love.

How is faith something that "remains"? And what, exactly, is faith?

Faith is belief. It is holding onto something greater than ourselves. During times of loss, it is essential to keep referring back to the developed beliefs that have carried us along in life. Sudden or severe loss may shake our beliefs, or we may discover there was something important missing from them. But beyond all that, we must hold on to and further develop any faith we had prior to the loss.

Some people find themselves thrust back onto some of their most basic beliefs, remembering even childhood prayers that comforted then and still comfort now.

Other people find that times of worship have heightened importance. They know something powerful is going on deep in their minds and hearts, and worship is a time when matters of the soul are respected and cultivated.

It is not unusual, on the other hand, for grieving people to find worship difficult. Sometimes it is because they have a hard time being around other people, but it may be just because their hearts feel raw—like they've been bruised and cut on the inside. They find themselves reacting to things that are said, feeling easily hurt or agitated. This is not very different from a person who has a broken foot and to whom any bump or pressure can feel excruciating. With time, the pain subsides. The injury heals.

Faith means stretching beyond ourselves and mooring our lives to something more stable than ourselves. Nobody adrift on the currents of life is in a safe position, much less when those currents turn into the violent waves of a storm of loss.

Those whose only mooring was a person they lost will face a severe faith crisis. They believed in a person, but people change, people leave, people die. It is never too late to find faith in something bigger than another person. People find new faith in God all the time.

The only reason faith can remain is that God remains. Faith in and of itself is the act of believing and trusting. The ropes that moor a boat alongside a secure dock are meaningless without the dock. So it is not faith itself that saves—it is God.

Faith is not an elaborate structure that we build with our own insight and ability, a tower reaching to God so we can have access. Quite the contrary, God has come to us in the person of Jesus Christ. Knowing that we are unable to find truth ourselves, God came to teach us. Since we are unable to reform ourselves, God came to change us. And because we lack the strength that we need to survive in a loss-filled world, God came to empower us.

For some people and at some times, faith is a strong shout of strong belief; at other times it is just a whisper for help. Either one will do because faith is simply the opening between our needy existence and God's superabundant grace.

Faith is built by listening to the voice of God. That's how all relationships of strong trust are built. The Bible, because it is God's own Word, is an expansive conversation between the God of heaven and the people God made to inhabit the earth. In the Scriptures, we find every conceivable kind of loss, real stories of real people who suffered:

- death and bereavement
- natural catastrophe
- betrayal
- loss of home
- loss of health
- loss of family
- loss of friendship
- loss of innocence
- loss of freedom

The Scriptures describe real human experiences. No matter what kind of loss we may suffer, we can find the same thing in the Bible. In it, we find scores of people who found ways to hold onto God when they went through times of severe loss. We may feel as though we need some guidance on the parts of the Bible to read when we are grieving, but we shouldn't be afraid to do it. The Psalms and the Gospel of John might be good places to read about why we go through what we do and what God has done to help us.

(adapted from *Life After Grief*, Mel Lawrenz and Daniel Green)

9

THINGS THAT REMAIN: HOPE

In that short list from 1 Corinthians 13:13 ("these three remain, faith, hope, and love"), the next is hope. After a difficult time of life, looking to the future can be one of the hardest things to do. Facing tomorrow or even getting through today can look foreboding, let alone the years that lie ahead.

Yet, hope is what allows us to face the future. It is the belief that we will be okay. It doesn't come to us out of thin air, and it is not wishful thinking. Some people tell others who are going through grief that they should just look on the bright side of things, but that is not hope. When people talk about "hoping for the best," it often doesn't get beyond a wish that the next roll of the dice won't be as bad as the last one. But true hope is based on something real.

If faith in God is what supports us from behind (as past experiences convince us of God's reality and goodness), then hope is what pulls us ahead (into our future).

Loss and distress are matters of the soul, touching us as deeply as any other experience. Numerous times in the Psalms, the question arises:

Why, my soul, are you downcast?

Why so disturbed within me?"

[To which the psalmist says:]

Put your hope in God,

for I will yet praise him,

my Savior and my God. (Ps. 42:5, 11; 43:5)

This kind of dialogue with the self is exactly like the push and pull of grief on the soul—on the one hand, a terrible inner aching and longing, on the other, a desire to survive, to look to tomorrow and not be afraid.

God knows how crippling grief and trauma can impact our experience. God knows mourners can feel so weak that they don't know how they can go on. And that is why many mourners find extraordinary strength in God. The prophet Isaiah said:

He gives strength to the weary

and increases the power of the weak.

Even youths grow tired and weary,

and young men stumble and fall;

but those who hope in the Lord

will renew their strength.

They will soar on wings like eagles;

they will run and not grow weary;

they will walk and not be faint (Isa. 40:29-31).

"Those who hope in the Lord." That means trusting that if God has done good things in the past, God will do so in the future. It means believing that God does not change. God is really the creator of the future. God is all about new beginnings, and sometimes a new future is molded with the best parts of the past. In other words, God does not demolish the past to begin a new future. Rather, God restores.

God's restoration comes in many ways. In the case of losing someone close to us, the things that we valued in that person remain valuable, and nobody can take them from us. The good memories we stored up in the past will go with us into the future. Those memories are more than just stored images or recorded information. They are parts of who we are, what shapes us today, and to that degree those memories are not imaginary. They are living and they are real. In fact, it is not just that the good and substantial parts of the past may carry on in the future, they almost inevitably will.

When we have warm memories of someone we've lost, it takes great effort to suppress them. Some people try to do that as a way of avoiding pain, but it usually fails. We can't evacuate ourselves of memories of the past, and we shouldn't try. That would only add loss on top of loss.

Then there is the kind of hope that goes beyond all others: hope of eternal life. Now, there are those who believe that when people die, they are at the absolute end. Death is irreparable loss, final silence. Most people living in most places at most times have believed otherwise. They have seen the incredible power of God-given life, the way that spiritual life transcends the merely material, and on that basis alone they have concluded that simple physical death couldn't possibly be the end. But there is more. The testimony of the authors of Scripture also points to eternal life beyond the lives we know now.

Heaven is never described in the Bible as people sprouting wings, donning white robes, sitting on clouds as they hear or play an endless strain of harp music (a state of affairs that, to some, seems more torturous than paradisal). No, heaven is not the comprehensive loss of everything we have held near and dear in this life, but the complete fulfillment of it all. Though beyond our comprehension, the new heaven and the new earth the Scriptures point to is the fullest measure of real relationships, real beauty, real goodness. It is so because the departed believer has drawn closer to the Creator of all good things than ever before.

For those whose lost loved one displayed no apparent faith in God, the funeral can be especially somber. Many mourners who have faith find themselves rehearsing the fact that "the Judge of all the earth [will] do right" (Gen. 18:25), and that, as mere mortals, we are not in a position to make eternal judgments. It is not possible for the mourner to hold on to the person who has died, but it is entirely possible, and necessary, for the mourner to hold on to God.

It is an extraordinary joy to be able to celebrate the living faith of someone who died in faith. Grief and mourning, tears and sobbing may still be there—these are not the denial of faith. But with faith is an otherworldly hope, a connection with the eternal, a link of future with future—that of the deceased who enjoys an improved existence in the presence of God, and the future of the mourners who know that God will carry them on in life.

That is the explanation of this statement of the apostle Paul: we "do not grieve like the rest of mankind, who have no hope" (1 Thess. 4:13). We will grieve loss (as did the giants of the faith and even Jesus himself), but it will not be a hopeless kind of grief.

Hope endures. And it helps us endure.

(adapted from *Life After Grief*, Mel Lawrenz and Daniel Green)

10

THINGS THAT REMAIN: LOVE

Everything in life changes, but a few things remain.

"These three remain: faith, hope, and love. But the greatest of these is love." 1 Corinthians 13 also says, "[Love] always protects, always trusts, always hopes, always perseveres. Love never fails."

There are, of course, many empty and half-hearted expressions of love. Sometimes people fall short of the love they claim to offer. Yet where there is real love, it has incredible enduring power and value, and for that reason it is able to help the mourner get through grief. Love does not dissipate because of distance. It is not shattered because of tension or temporary conflict. It perseveres when there are difficulties.

When loss occurs, love is not ruined. We may lose a loved one but not lose the love. Death cannot bury memories of love. Love is what turns memories from mere mental data into warm, living remembrances. Like faith and hope, love is one of those experiences of life that remains. It is another mooring available when we feel like a storm surge is pressing hard against us. Like faith and hope, love remains because it is one of the links that we have with God.

Real love is essentially a spiritual resource. It is not borne of human invention and initiative. The Bible teaches that we are capable of love only because it is who God is.

Love comes from God: "Everyone who loves has been born of God and knows God. Whoever does not love does not know God, because God is love . . . . No one has ever seen God; but if we love one another, God lives in us and his love is made complete in us" (1 John 4:7-8, 12).

On the day Moses received a revelation of God on Mt. Sinai, the event revealed the core nature of God as holy love. "The Lord, the Lord, the compassionate and gracious God, slow to anger, abounding in love and faithfulness, maintaining love to thousands, and forgiving wickedness, rebellion and sin" (Ex. 34:6-7).

No wonder real love has such enduring value. It would not be an exaggeration to say that love is who God is; it is why God made us; it is the substance of good human relationships; it is the reason that life is a process of gain as well as loss. If we are made in the image of

God, as Genesis says, and if God is love, as Scripture widely attests, then love is one of those qualities overlapping the divine and the human.

If we did not love, we would not hurt when we lose someone close to us. And the opposite is true: if you want to protect yourself from any sense of grieving, if you want to avoid ever having to be a mourner, then don't let yourself love. But if you make that choice, you will cut yourself off from who God is and who humankind is intended to be. You may avoid the sense of loss, but only because you have caused yourself to lose what is most important in life.

How do we find God's help when we grieve? We ask God to show us what it is that remains even in the face of devastating loss. And much does remain. We ask God to strengthen our faith, lengthen our hope, and deepen our love.

When Jesus himself faced the loneliness and desolation of his own imminent death, he asked several of his friends to abide with him, to remain. His words, embellished by a hymn writer, have often been sung as a prayer by people in need asking God to remain:

Abide with me, fast falls the eventide;
The darkness deepens; Lord with me abide!
When other helpers fail and comforts flee,
Help of the helpless, oh, abide with me.

A BETTER YEAR AHEAD?

(adapted from *Life After Grief*, Mel Lawrenz and Daniel Green)

11

LIVING IN THE PRESENT

A lot of us deal with worry. When someone says, "You shouldn't worry so much," our first thought is: "Easy to say, but look around. There is plenty to worry about!"

For some people, worry is real anxiety, an always-near sense of tension, agitation, and fear. The Bible never says that worry and anxiety are sins, or even that they show a lack of faith. Yet Jesus made statement in the Sermon on the Mount, so familiar to us: "Therefore I tell you, do not worry about your life, what you will eat or drink; or about your body, what you will wear" (Matt. 6:25).

What, exactly, did he mean?

Jesus was addressing some of the universal pressing questions we all ask: *Who is going to take care of me? Will I be able to endure this period of my life? Could next year be better than the last?*

The answer?

"Your heavenly Father knows you need them," (i.e. food, drink, and clothing) so don't get caught in the rat race or, we might say, the pagan chase ("the pagans run after all these things") (Matt. 6:32). We can do better than living a life of desperate grabbing. Our security does not come from how much money we have in the bank or from the brand names of our clothing. Having enough food in the house is a good thing. But no matter how much any of us have to eat or drink or wear or drive or store, we will never know security until we trust in the love of God. God knows what we have and what we need. God also knows, more than we do, what we need. What we *really* need.

Sparrows do fall to the ground. But not one of them falls to the ground apart from the care of God the Father (Matt. 10:29). A lot of us are like birds with broken wings right now. We don't travel or get out as much as we used to. This year might be a time when we see loved ones ill or even pass away. But this is not new in human history. Life is an ongoing pattern of both gain and loss.

The reality of pain and loss does not nullify providence. Goodness is always greater than evil as surely as light is greater than darkness. The only reasonable explanation for why our lives work at all is that the Creator of all things keeps everything going day by day.

There are many things that could go wrong with my body right now, but at the moment it seems to be working just fine. My meals are being converted from fuel to energy and my lungs are taking in air and putting life-giving oxygen into my blood. My brain is firing away, directing every function in my body, and my heart is beating without pause, pushing lifeblood to every part of my body. I've been ill before, and I know I'll be ill again. Actually, I'm astonished that my body works as well as it does. The function of my body is the ongoing, providential work of God.

Our lungs and hearts don't always work right, and sooner or later they all stop. The world has continual international conflicts and wars. Every moment of the day, someone somewhere is perpetrating a serious crime against someone else. Horrible things go on behind closed doors.

But all wicked acts and personal injuries are set against the backdrop of so many healthy days, good relationships, and proper exchanges. Kindness, forgiveness, forbearance, generosity, patience: these are signs that God keeps gifting us. The irrepressible good things that happen in life come about because the God who gave us life is a good God.

Rain keeps falling, living things keep growing, and the human race keeps reaching out for hope and life. In some ways, the creation keeps asserting itself. It is alive, even though drought and disease and death are inevitable. The

Creator keeps giving good things. God keeps saying, *I've made what I've made. I will keep it going and growing and re-create as the need arises.*

So, when Jesus says, "do not worry about your life," he is not telling us to play a game in which we ignore loss or pain—he himself experienced distress and sorrow and tension. Instead, Jesus is reforming our security. He is saying that anxiety about food and clothing, or about pursuing status in the eyes of the world, will not actually deliver security and comfort. There is a better way.

12

REVERENCE AND RESPECT

On one occasion an expert in the law stood up to test Jesus. "Teacher," he asked, "what must I do to inherit eternal life?"

"What is written in the Law?" he replied. "How do you read it?"

He answered, "'Love the Lord your God with all your heart and with all your soul and with all your strength and with all your mind'; and, 'Love your neighbor as yourself.'"

"You have answered correctly," Jesus replied. "Do this and you will live."

(Luke 10:25-28)

If you are looking for a set of values that will support dignity in your life, connect you with the life of God, and work at a practical level, you need look no further than these: *reverence* and *respect*.

Reverence happens in our hearts when we are exposed to the power and majesty of God. Reverence (Latin: *reverentia*) means awe. Wonder. Esteem. Even fear.

Reverence is the prophet saying, "Woe to me... I am a man of unclean lips" (Isa. 6:5). It is the newly-called disciple of Jesus saying, "Go away from me, Lord; I am a sinful man!" (Luke 5:8). It is the submissive apostle saying, "Oh, the depth of the riches of the wisdom and knowledge of God! How unsearchable his judgments, and his paths beyond tracing out!" (Rom. 11:33).

The purpose of worship is for us to be awe-filled to the point that we are driven to submission to God. The main word for worship in the Greek New Testament means "to bend the knee." So every act of worship—praise, prayer, offering, the reading and exposition of Scripture, baptism, the Lord's Supper—is most effective when it leads to awe. That awe is not confined to a church building. We can, and must, stay bowed before God in the workplace, at school, in our families.

We turn to the horizontal. *Reverence* (for God) leads to *respect* (for people).

The most important thing you can do for the people in your life—your family, your friends, your co-workers—is to treat them with respect. The reason we love is because we respect. We react to God's greatness with reverence, then we turn around and look at these amazing creatures God has made in his own image (in his own image!)—men and women, boys and girls—and we treat them with respect because they are made in God's image. The alternative is unthinkable; to slap the image of God in the face is to slap God himself.

One thing every person wants is respect. *Every* person. If we want people to grow, we will respect them. If we hope people will find security and confidence, we will respect them. If we long to see the people in our lives have a life-giving connection with God, we will respect them.

Respect is a choice we make. It does not come naturally to us. The easy thing is to use or abuse other people, after all, we're busy. We have things to do, places to go, goals to achieve. (How dare other people get in our way or make our lives complicated!)

The word "respect" literally means to take another look. "Re-spect"—to look again. Given the coarseness of our culture, it is time to stop and take another look.

It is never too late for us to say to God, *Give me a new vision of the people around me. Help me to see them as you see them.*

So, we take another look. And another look. And another, over time. Re-spect, and re-spect again. We get to know people, really know them. Only then are we able to respond in truth.

This is consistent with Jesus saying that the whole Law is summed up in one simple truth with two parts: "Love the Lord your God [reverence]... and love your neighbor as yourself [respect]" (Luke 10:27). Jesus said, "do this, and you will live."

Following this truth does cost us a great deal. Looking at God with reverence takes away all our bragging rights (which we never had in the first place), and respecting people—taking another look—means our treatment of others will have to be more careful, more discerning, and more generous than we ever imagined.

If we long for a better year ahead, it is within our power. If we just imagine for a moment millions of people deciding that respecting each other is not only a good thing, it is the right thing, what difference would that make in our society? If we imagine millions more people realizing that reverence for the Creator of all is the smart thing to do, we will find ourselves side by side, on our knees, looking up.

That's better than shooting at each other, or spewing hate toward each other, or trashing each other.

It will make for a better year.

PRAYER

Praise to God the Father

(audio version at www.wordway.org/audioprayers)

Holy Father in heaven, how grateful we are for your great power and providence. You are not like the phantom gods which human beings have fabricated. You are the one and only true God, not a lie.

O Father, you are great and you are good.

Great because you are Spirit.

Great because you exist before all things.

Great because you are the living God and are the author of life.

Great because you are the personal God, the God of Abraham, of Isaac, and of Jacob

—not the God of empty philosophy.

Great because you know all things.

Great because you are Almighty.

Great because you are present everywhere.

Great because you do not change.

Father, you are great, and you are good. Else we would be in danger.

Good because you are holy.

Good because you are righteous.

Good because you are just.

Good because you are love.

Good because you are truth.

Your greatness and goodness, O Father, exceed our comprehension. But any day we catch a glimmer of your glory, our lives are better.

We have been prodigals, Father. We want to come home. We want to stay at home.

Amen.

(from *Prayers for Our Lives: 95 Lifelines to God for Everyday Circumstances* by Mel Lawrenz)

13

PRAYER AS DAILY DIALOGUE WITH GOD

Prayer is best when it is a continual dialogue with God over the course of the day. Someone once said, "I do not often pray for 15 minutes straight, but hardly ever do 15 minutes pass without me praying." In other words, praying does not require us to go to a special room, get down on our knees, and stay there until our legs cramp. Rather, anyone can say a sentence or two to God anytime, day or night, anywhere, out loud or silently.

If we pray many times as the day unfolds, it develops in us a steady heart-openness to God. We are responding to God the moment we see any special act or blessing from him. We are asking God questions during the day—the whole day—about what we're experiencing, the decisions we're making, the words we choose.

The day may look like this…

You wake up and you immediately begin thinking about what you'll be doing, so you say to God: *Thank you for the chance to rest and to start again. Please help me see you in this day and please you by who I am today.*

You shower and, as you relax, all kinds of thoughts pop into your head. Some worries, some regrets, some ideas. You say to God: *Please take my concerns today. I leave them in your hands, and I ask for guidance for the choices I have to make. Help me know what I should do.*

You take 15 or 20 minutes in a quiet part of the house to read a chapter or two in the Bible, saying first to God: *Open my eyes, gracious Lord, as I turn to your Word. I long to know you, to understand life, and to be changed. Examine me, Lord, by the floodlight of your truth. Amen.*

After you read from the Bible, you take some time to let the words sink in, then pray: *May the word I have read, Lord, be planted deeply in my mind and heart. Help me not to walk away and forget it, but to meditate on it and obey it and so build my life on the rock of your truth. Amen.*

As you start your tasks for the day, you ask God for guidance and protection. You pray: *Help me to believe in your presence throughout this day.*

You're in a tense conversation with someone. You have to decide what to say and when to hold your tongue. You pray silently: *Lord, give me the right words.*

The weather is good, so you go out for a walk. You breathe in the fresh air, you have a chance to clear your head, and every so often you say something aloud or silently to God. You're reminded of something good, so you thank God. A regret comes to mind, so you express that to God. You feel a burden for a family member, so you ask God for help.

As the day wears on, you cast a silent or verbal sentence to God during many situations. It is almost like you are talking to a friend. But you always remember that this is the Lord of heaven and earth you are talking to, and you welcome the sense of reverence that brings.

The day is done, and you're about to go to bed.

You pray:

Dear Lord, I am thinking about the good and challenging things that happened today. There is always so much of life that is outside of my control, and I don't always make the best choices with what I do control.

Once again, I'm glad you allow me to live in a steady stream of your mercy. I would be completely lost without you.

I need rest now, so I commit my mind, body, and spirit to you. I rest in you.

In Jesus' name. Amen.

PRAYER

Praise to Christ the Lord

(audio version at www.wordway.org/audioprayers)

Lord Jesus Christ, we adore you and praise you. Where would we be without you? We long to live in your glory and your goodness.

You identified yourself with God the Father when you said "I am." You explained your life and purpose by saying...

"I am the bread of life" —and so we know we live through you.

"I am the light of the world" —and so we no longer live in the darkness of evil and ignorance.

"I am the gate for the sheep" —and so we know we are protected from spiritual predators.

"I am the good shepherd" —and so we are well fed, and led, and protected.

"I am the resurrection and the life" —and so we can live above the fear of illness and death.

"I am the way, the truth, and the life" —and so we see a clear way forward toward abundant life.

"I am the true vine" —and so we know staying connected to you is the most important priority we must have.

Lord Jesus, you are "the author of life." You came so that we may have life, and have it to the full.

We can stand before God the Father because of your great sacrifice. You made peace through the blood of your cross, in order to reconcile all things to yourself.

We are overwhelmed. We are in awe. We are humbled. We wish to worship and follow you all the days of our lives. We want to know you—yes, to know the power of your resurrection and participation in your sufferings, becoming like you in your death, and so, somehow, attaining to the resurrection from the dead.

Amen.

(from *Prayers for Our Lives: 95 Lifelines to God for Everyday Circumstances* by Mel Lawrenz)

14

TAKING IN THE LIVING WORD

Early in life, I thought the Bible was a good guide to living and protection from danger, like the guardrails along a dangerous road. But that is a stunted view of what Scripture has to offer. Living the Bible means that the essential qualities of our lives are shaped by the truth of God. It is about life itself.

Living the Bible, in other words, is about the Bible—the Word of God—living in us. It is a living Word, because it contains life and prompts life.

As the psalmist puts it, the person who delights in God's Word is "like a tree planted by streams of water, which yields its fruit in season and whose leaf does not wither" (Ps. 1:3). The tree is not planted automatically. It is all too easy for us to read the Word of God with no effect whatsoever if we just look at the Bible as a pile of facts. Or maybe we long for a time when Scripture impacted us deeply, but that has faded recently and we wonder why. We all know people who need a spark of spiritual life or the protection of the truth of God's Word, but they look down upon the Bible. It is almost like they think the Bible is trying to take something away from them, rather than give them life.

One day, Jesus explained to his disciples why some people receive the message of the kingdom of God and others do not, using a comparison from the natural world as he often did. A sower goes out to plant a crop, casting seed this way and that. Some of the seed lands on the hard-packed path the sower is walking on, some falls onto soil that is thin because of rocks and stones, some of the seed falls among wild plants like thorn bushes, and some actually lands in good, fertile soil where it has a chance to sprout, grow, and produce. Jesus then explains the meaning of his parable, point by point.

Listen then to what the parable of the sower means: When anyone hears the message about the kingdom and does not understand it, the evil one comes and snatches away what was sown in their heart. This is the seed sown along the path. The seed falling on rocky ground refers to someone who hears the word and at once receives it with joy. But since they have no root, they last only a short time. When trouble or persecution comes because of the word, they quickly fall away. The seed falling among the thorns refers to someone who hears the word, but the worries of this life and the deceitfulness of wealth choke the word, making it unfruitful. But the seed falling on good soil refers to someone who hears the word and understands it. This is the one who produces a crop, yielding a hundred, sixty or thirty times what was sown. (Matt. 13:18-23)

This is assumed in the parable: the seed is good. It has all the potential for life and fruitfulness. The variable in the parable is the soil—our receptiveness to God's words.

When we do not let God's messages in, like a hard surface on which seeds will bounce (the path), absolutely nothing will happen. In fact, a hard and stubborn heart is exactly what the Evil One wants.

When we listen to the Word of God but only let it penetrate in a shallow way (the rocky ground), the effects are superficial and temporary.

"The worries of this life and the deceitfulness of wealth" (the thorns) form stories told many times over. Someone wants to have a living faith in God and may even enjoy that life for a little while, but it is short-lived against the competition of worries and materialism. We see it in celebrity believers who speak about faith for a while, until it fades away. Ordinary people experience it all the time. "The worries of this life" applies when we spend large amounts of time accumulating more material goods. We are free to do that, but we'll have chosen one master over another.

Then there is the good soil. In times past when my wife and I planted a garden in the spring, the first task was soil preparation. Do it well, with rich soil, some peat moss for aeration, and a bit of natural fertilizer—mix it all together, and you can scoop up handfuls of rich-smelling soil. You know the seed is going to love that soil.

Living the Bible is an organic process. It is about a living Word deeply taking root until eventually we are amazed at the harvest. This will not happen if we view the Bible as merely a book of rules.

Some self-examination is in order here. Are we ready to receive the Word of God like good soil, or do things like our worry and financial stress compete with the truth of God? Are we letting the Word of God develop deep roots, or are we being shallow with it? Are we guarding against hard hearts, which won't receive the truth of God at all?

15

WISDOM OR FOOLISHNESS?

If you had a difficult decision to make today that was complicated and would affect the rest of your life, what kind of person would you go to for advice? You'd be smart if you sought out people whom you know to have a lot of wisdom.

Most people are longing for wisdom, whether they use the word or not. When they get advice that has a ring of truth to it, and it leads them to goodness and wholeness and peace, they are deeply satisfied. Most people wish their leaders were wiser. There are just too many ways in which a lack of wisdom, or outright foolishness, can hurt ourselves and others.

What is wisdom? Both a special gift from God and a personal skill that is developed over time, wisdom is deep insight into the true nature of things, including their moral value, and the integrity to act on that insight. Wisdom is not different from knowledge but is more than knowledge—like the difference between knowing about your spouse and knowing your spouse.

The Bible is a book full of wisdom, and it teaches that God wants every person to grow in wisdom. This is the highest form of drawing on the Word of God—to grow deeper and deeper in wisdom, to gain "the wisdom from above" (James 3:17), and "the mind of Christ" (1 Cor. 2:16). Then our life choices, large and small, will be good and right because they have been regulated by the moral quality that is at the heart of God's wisdom.

The alternative is unthinkable. The book of Proverbs speaks about "the fool," but there are several different levels of foolishness, marked by the Hebrew words that are used.

The most primitive form of foolishness is *simplemindedness*. This is simple ignorance. Not knowing any better. Making mistakes. Being naive. Simplemindedness can cause great harm, but more serious still is the second kind of foolishness: *carelessness*. We are careless when we choose not to listen to good advice, when we rush a decision, when we say or do things without regard for their effects on other people, when we are foolish through negligence. That can cause a lot of harm. The strongest form of foolishness in the book of Proverbs is *cynicism and hypocrisy*. This is the "scoffer," someone who mocks what is good. When people just give up on integrity, or act civilly in public but turn into monsters behind closed doors, that is the strongest form of foolishness.

The Apostle Paul told the Corinthians, "When I came to you, I did not come with eloquence or human wisdom as I proclaimed to you the testimony about God" (1 Cor. 2:1). He said, "I resolved to know nothing while I was with you except Jesus Christ and him crucified" (1 Cor. 2:2). Jesus is the message. He is better than "the wisdom of this age or of the rulers of this age, who are coming to nothing" (1 Cor. 2:6).

And so, Paul says, "This is what we speak, not in words taught us by human wisdom but in words taught by the Spirit, explaining spiritual realities with Spirit-taught words" (1 Cor. 2:13).

So, how does this work? How can we live out the wisdom of Scripture?

First, we must read all of Scripture with open and teachable minds. Every page has wisdom, and we will catch different points over the years.

Then we can pay special attention to the so-called "wisdom literature" of the Bible. Anybody would do well to read the remarkable book of Proverbs once a year. Its opening words speak of its purpose:

Proverbs […] for gaining wisdom and instruction;
    for understanding words of insight;
  for receiving instruction in prudent behavior,
    doing what is right and just and fair;
  for giving prudence to those who are simple,

knowledge and discretion to the young—
let the wise listen and add to their learning,
    and let the discerning get guidance. (Prov. 1:1-5)

The book of Proverbs gives us general statements of what is true—this is different from God's promises. The book of Proverbs makes us wiser in how we view life. It shapes our expectations so they are not too low or high. It also gives us bold warnings about dangerous life decisions.

The book of James in the New Testament focuses a lot on wisdom. It, too, offers practical advice about life. In contrast with "earthly wisdom" which is so misguided that it leads to "envy and selfish ambition," "disorder," "and every evil practice," James says "the wisdom that comes from heaven is first of all pure; then peace-loving, considerate, submissive, full of mercy and good fruit, impartial and sincere" (James 3:16,17).

Each quality on that list describes both attitude and action. Live a life of deeper wisdom, and people will seek you out. You will have the blessing of helping people avoid cliffs and move on to good places in their lives.

PRAYER

Asking God for Wisdom

"But the wisdom that comes from heaven is first of all pure; then peace-loving, considerate, submissive, full of mercy and good fruit, impartial and sincere."
James 3:17

Dear God, I need your higher wisdom. The wisdom of this world is not enough. It is not strong enough, it is not good enough, it is not steady enough.

The wisdom you give is "pure," dear God. You know my inner motives better than I do. You know my good motives, my bad motives, and my mixed motives. Purify me, that I may be wiser.

The wisdom you give is "peace-loving." Help me to cherish peace, to live in peace, and to be a peacemaker for others.

The wisdom you give is "considerate." Help me not to be selfish, unsympathetic, ungracious, impolite, or rude toward others, especially those I am closest to. Give me a caring spirit.

The wisdom you give is "submissive." I know I am sometimes stubborn and unyielding. Sometimes I think I know more than I do. Grant me a teachable spirit. *Help me to cooperate with others rather than just trying to get my way.*

The wisdom you give is "full of mercy and good fruit." Help me to have mercy toward others while still holding on to your truth. Guide me into acts of mercy that will be fruitful.

The wisdom you give is "impartial." Make me a fair-minded person, Lord. I admit I often act out of my own biases. Raise me above my preferences. Make me truthful and make me fair so that I can help others.

The wisdom you give is "sincere," gracious Lord. I admit to being hypocritical at times. I know I am not always honest in what I say. I regret that sometimes others don't trust me. I long for the freedom that comes from truthfulness.

Lord, help me find others who have "the wisdom that comes from heaven," and to learn from them. And may others find that in me.

Amen.

(from *Prayers for Our Lives: 95 Lifelines to God for Everyday Circumstances* by Mel Lawrenz)

16

BEING A DISCERNING PERSON

Life is complicated. Every day we face decisions, large and small, that can be knotty and convoluted. Make a poor choice and we may suffer for it or others may be hurt. If we're smart, we'll realize we need wisdom that we can gain from trusted, mature friends and from the Scriptures, God's deposit of wisdom for us.

God's wisdom is not merely a collection of trustworthy principles for life. Wisdom includes a developed ability to make good judgments between what is right and wrong, or good, better, and best. It is what the Bible calls discernment, and it can save us from disaster.

Charles Spurgeon said, "Discernment is not a matter of simply telling the difference between right and wrong;" rather, it is "knowing the difference between right and almost right." Discernment, in other words, is refined perception. It is an ability to see, at a deep level, our own strengths and weaknesses and those of others. Discernment helps us know what our true motives are.

The New Testament word for discernment (*diakrina*) means to separate or distinguish. Discernment is the ability to cut carefully between what is good and bad. A surgeon takes a scalpel in hand in order to cut a line between healthy and diseased tissue. We want our surgeons to be skilled so that they don't leave behind disease and they don't cut away what is healthy. We want them to use good quality scalpels, not butter knives.

Discernment helps us to be discriminating without being discriminatory. To judge without being judgmental. To separate without dividing. Discernment is fine work.

When we are discerning, we are less likely to make foolish decisions based on rash evaluations of our situation. We will not take a black-and-white view of things, a tendency in our society today that comes from simple laziness. Bias is the easy way. Discernment respects others and honors God.

Hebrews 4:12 describes how the Scriptures are the scalpel God has gifted us: "The word of God is alive and active. Sharper than any double-edged sword, it penetrates even to dividing soul and spirit, joints and marrow; it judges the thoughts and attitudes of the heart."

Generally, we should avoid judging the hearts of others because only God knows the heart. If we don't want other people to assume they know our motives, we have to withhold from judging the motives of others. Jesus said, "Do not judge, or you too will be judged. For in the same way you judge others, you will be judged, and with the measure you use, it will be measured to you" (Matt. 7:1–2).

On the other hand, we are called to exercise judgment. "Do you not know that the Lord's people will judge the world? And if you are to judge the world, are you not competent to judge trivial cases? Do you not know that we will judge angels? How much more the things of this life!" (1 Cor. 6:2-3).

So, what is the difference between exercising judgment and being judgmental? We are being judgmental when our motive is to devalue or control others, or to be self-righteous as a matter of pride.

Note that Hebrews 4:12 speaks of God's Word as alive and active. The Word of God penetrates even into the inner recesses of our hearts. Scalpels cut, but with the purpose of eventual healing. We are not to apply verses of the Bible, in other words, in mechanical and crude ways to our lives or in judgment of others. The Word of God develops a living dynamic in our hearts whereby our instincts and perceptions are trained. We can see sin over the horizon when we are tempted. We are able to sense when someone is lying to us or to themselves. We can spot the difference between a counterfeit and the real thing.

Hebrews 5:14 speaks of mature believers "who by constant use have trained themselves to distinguish good from evil." The ability to discern comes by training; there is no substitute for accumulated experience. A surgeon gets better and better with the repetition of the same procedures, and by reading professional literature as a habit. In the same way, we get better and better at discerning the complexities of life through experience and by a lifestyle of reading Scripture.

Living a life of discernment means that we exercise a kind of penetrating vision that helps us see through the dust and fog of life, to see things the way they really are, and to make conscious choices about the people we want to influence us. Discernment is perception, insight, and correct judgment about the people wanting to influence us.

Discernment is about living in reality rather than random imagination or someone else's lie. The alternative—to live in some degree of self-deception or extreme naiveté—is not right and certainly not safe.

17

CONVICTION AND TOLERANCE

One of the tensions we face today is that many people have aligned themselves with a group of people who have the same attitude and values, and the commitment becomes absolute. There is no open-mindedness to other points of view, no real dialogue. People form tribes, and they believe their mission is to make war on other tribes.

But Scripture calls us to two dynamics: conviction *and* tolerance. We can exercise both. And we are called to do so.

Real convictions aren't just a lot of noise—they accomplish something. It was an imprisoned Paul, persecuted by the Roman and Jewish authorities, criticized and sometimes undermined by other Christians, who said that he remained unashamed of the convictions he was living for and willing to die for (Rom. 1:16).

Conviction is not simply the brusqueness of stout-hearted personalities. It is not a characteristic of temperament. Some people with the strongest of convictions are actually quite unassuming, unpretentious, even meek. Like strong and stable oak trees, their roots go deep, having found the sources of life way beneath the surface of things. Anybody can have convictions, because anybody can be gripped by conviction itself.

Belief has power in that it gives life. We are saved through belief in the truth (2 Thess. 2:13), a salvation that includes more than a promise of paradise. Belief in the truth has a saving effect because it delivers us from our ignorance, our limitations, and our failings. An ever-clearer picture of reality—which belief brings—makes a more profound practical difference in a person's life than anything else.

Conviction leads to life-giving sacrifice. Why would we, why should we, give up our time, our money, our convenience, or comfort? Why sacrifice security or even one's life? The only explanation for that whole range of sacrifices, from simple giving to martyrdom, is conviction. Belief in the living God means being owned by another, borne along by a network of principles that preceded your birth and will continue in force as inherent laws of the universe after you die. It is to be a part of something so much larger than yourself. Does life make sense any other way?

Conviction is not only demanding, but generous as well. If it entails obedience and sacrifice, it also provides the spiritual protection we need to live in a spiritually dangerous world. Why is it that "the armor of God" from Ephesians 6 is so memorable? Could it be that we are aware of our profound insecurity in our inner lives without some defensive and offensive capabilities? Most of the pieces of this armor are derivatives of conviction: the belt of truth, the breastplate of righteousness, the shield of faith, the sword which is the Word of God.

Courage arises from conviction. Fear of the world is not the appropriate stance of believers. Some of the most fearful believers are parents. Knowing the vulnerability of these unformed lives, there is a temptation to isolate them from the world rather than instill in them the personal belief system that will be their armor. Yet, if you study the convictions of children, you may be amazed and realize that we should never underestimate the power of the beliefs held in the smaller hearts of the community of faith.

And then there is the call to tolerance.

The Bible insists that, though Christians are to be people of conviction, they are also to be models of tolerance. Conviction is brittle and harsh when someone shows little ability or inclination to tolerance. Conviction without tolerance is a closed system, insensitive to outside ideas or different kinds of people. It cannot grow because of its own self-confinement. Tolerance is humility, sensitivity, openness, teachability. It is knowing that you do not know everything and taking the posture of a learner.

Paul summarizes this well:

Therefore, as God's chosen people, holy and dearly loved, clothe yourselves with compassion, kindness, humility, gentleness and patience. Bear with each other and forgive one another if any of you has a grievance against someone. Forgive as the Lord forgave you. And over all these virtues put on love, which binds them all together in perfect unity. (Col. 3:12-14)

A balanced attitude toward God and toward other people will always combine the stability of conviction and the openness of tolerance. To be a disciple is to know the master whom you follow and to have an open ear to the things you have not yet learned, even things that may fly in the face of your earlier beliefs or prejudices.

PRAYER

Praise to the Holy Spirit

(audio version at www.wordway.org/audioprayers)

Come, Holy Spirit, come.

Since you came as the "advocate" Jesus spoke about, the world has never been the same. And so we ask now:

Fill us with your awe-inspiring glory.

Empower us for the great mission to which we are called.

Pour out your love and your gifts.

Enlighten us with the truth of the word of God.

Grant us the righteousness, peace, and joy that your presence brings.

Purify us through your sanctifying work.

Protect us, Holy Spirit, so that we do not grieve you, or quench you, or resist you.

We want to keep in step with you, Holy Spirit. We need a lifelong fellowship with you. May our lives show the fruit of your presence, transforming us into people of love, joy, peace, patience, kindness, goodness, faithfulness, gentleness, and self control.

Come, Holy Spirit, come.

A BETTER YEAR AHEAD?

(from *Prayers for Our Lives: 95 Lifelines to God for Everyday Circumstances* by Mel Lawrenz)

18

DEALING WITH DOUBT

Doubt is not the opposite of belief—it is simply the horizon between what we know with certainty today and what we hope becomes clearer in the future. I am glad when I have the opportunity to speak with people who have doubts about their faith, because that is what Jesus spent a lot of his time doing.

Christopher Hitchens, now deceased, doubted that God exists. Actually, that's a huge understatement. Hitchens, a noted journalist and literary critic, positively disbelieved in the existence of God. And he wanted to disbelieve. On a television talk show, Hitchens told NBC journalist Tim Russert that he didn't believe in God because he thought there was no evidence for it, and went on to say:

I don't want it to be the case, that there is a divine superintending celestial dictatorship from which I could never escape and that abolishes my private life . . . that would supervise me, keep me under surveillance in every moment of my living existence. And then, when I died, it would be like living in a heavenly North Korea where one's only duty was to continue to abase oneself and to thank forever the dear leader for everything that we are and have.

Hitchens did not believe and said straight out that he didn't *want* to believe in God—because he didn't want to live under a scrutinizing divine dictatorship. But who would want to believe in a graceless, loveless, arbitrary God? Hitchens rejected an idea of God that *ought* to be rejected.

His book *God Is Not Great: How Religion Poisons Everything* got everybody's attention as soon as it was published. Hitchens may not have believed in a great God, but he profited immensely from writing a bestseller about the non-existence of a great God. The book is disbelief written in language that is as big and as blunt as can be. The title says it all. It's not that Hitchens, a thoughtful and articulate person, was incapable of nuance, but this book is so extreme that it's hard to take his main point seriously. Anyone with half a brain would have to admit that sometimes religion poisons things—but only if it is a variety that is poisonous. It's hardly fair to take torture in the Inquisition, radical Islamic jihad, and fringe practices of ultra-orthodox Jews and say, "This is where religion will get you; this is what it is all about." It isn't logical or reasonable. Atheism is Hitchens's chosen commitment—but, while he may point out that many atheists and rationalists are well-behaved, he should not ignore the cruelties of the atheistic regimes of Stalin, Pol Pot, and Hitler. A logical interpretation of history dictates that you cannot judge Christianity (or other religions) based on their worst-case manifestations—and you cannot take some examples of good-natured, well-meaning atheists as an endorsement of the complete rejection of God.

Some people—not many—are absolute in their disbelief (by Hitchens's own estimation, probably only 2 percent of people in the U.S. hold to his brand of complete atheism). The vast majority of people are believers in some sense and carry on in life with a conviction of the presence and the goodness of God. But what do we say about the experience of doubt? What is it? Why does it happen? What can a person do with nagging doubt? Is doubt a sin against God?

I am glad when I have the opportunity to speak with people who have doubts about their faith. Don't get me wrong—I'm not glad about the pain that they experience in one of the most intimate issues of life. That pain can be intense—like that felt by a husband or wife who overhears whispering hints that his or her spouse has been cheating, or like the pain that follows the death of a loved one. Conversations with people who doubt are often halting, quiet, scattered. I have never met someone of faith who wanted to have doubts about their faith, because it really isn't about doubting faith—it's about doubting God. People don't want to doubt God; they just have questions that come up in life that hang in the air like half-inflated helium balloons. Sometimes they feel like they can't look past them—they want some answers.

For many, doubt is like driving into a fog. You didn't see it coming, but now you're in it. You don't know how to get out of it, you don't know what way to turn, and you don't even remember exactly where you were when you got into it. You didn't ask for the fog—it's just how things are.

The reason I say I'm glad for those conversations is that it is better for someone experiencing doubt to talk about it than to let doubt fester. Like grief, doubt itself does not injure; it is often the result of injury. And we need to know this: our doubts do not injure God, because nothing can injure God. It is possible to insult God—because any of us are capable of disrespect—but doubt in the form of sincere questioning is not an insult to God. The Bible never says that the moment we waver, God is ready to cut us off. The Bible is one long story of human beings living on the horizon between faith and doubt, interacting with their Creator—all the time showing their inclination: "I want to believe." Doubt is not a contradiction of faith. It is its precursor.

Ultimately, the question we need to answer is: How are we going to deal with doubt? The answer is different for the habitual doubt of the utter skeptic and for the passing doubt of the believer who has been tossed into uncertainty because of a life crisis. But in either case, the only effective response to doubt is to get rooted in real faith.

There is a passionate plea in the middle of the book of Colossians in the New Testament, in which the apostle Paul says:

Just as you received Christ Jesus as Lord, continue to live [literally, "walk"] in him, rooted and built up in him, strengthened in the faith as you were taught, and overflowing with thankfulness.

See to it that no one takes you captive through hollow and deceptive philosophy, which depends on human tradition and the basic principles of this world rather than on Christ.

For in Christ all the fullness of the Deity lives in bodily form, and you have been given fullness in Christ, who is the head over every power and authority. (Col. 2:6-10)

There is nothing better that can happen to a person in life than to come to the place of saying "I believe." It is like someone turns the lights on or, better yet, the day has dawned and the confusion and oppression of the darkness of life has been pushed back.

We want to believe because, without faith, all we're left with is a gigantic question mark about the meaning and purpose of life, no real hope for the future, and no assurance that we are loved by anyone beyond passing human affection. Without faith, we are cut off from our Creator and, consequently, cut off from what He has created. All of life becomes disjointed. It is like sitting on a stool with two of the three legs loose—the whole thing could collapse at any moment.

If we want to believe, then we need to realize that faith doesn't happen in a moment; it is a lifelong walk. Those who receive Jesus as Lord need to begin and continue a walk with Him. When you put these two ideas together—receiving and walking—you get a total picture of faith. It is not just walking, as if it were up to us to go on a great quest in order to find God who is hidden up high in the mountains somewhere; but neither is it only receiving, which would be like repeating vows in a wedding ceremony but not following through with marital commitment.

Many believers are fond of speaking in terms of "receiving" Christ, and that is biblical, as we see in the passage from Colossians. But it is only one way of describing the reality of faith. And it is important that we realize just how serious this receiving is. It is not merely saying the right words or praying the right prayer as if they were some kind of incantation. While it is true that the front end of receiving the Lord Jesus is a simple admission of need—a plea for mercy, an opening of heart and hands—we should realize that receiving a lord means to give up one's own lordship of life. (And we would do well to eliminate from our vocabulary the phrase "making Christ Lord." We don't make Him anything. If Jesus Christ is Lord, He is Lord whether we acknowledge it or not.)

Then the walk begins. Just one step after another, not worrying about whether or not you'll make it to the top of the mountain of life, because God will inevitably have to carry you some of the way and will bring you to the summit in the end.

How do you deal with doubt? You tell yourself that you're not inventing faith, that you don't have to have all of life's questions answered today, that you don't need to figure out exactly where you will be five years from now. God knows. You just have to take the next step.

Now, to switch metaphors, there is tremendous assurance that if you are on the walk of faith with Christ as Lord, you're doing the right thing because you have been "rooted and built up" and "strengthened." Every time you have the sense of being uprooted by some tornado that has come through your life—a sudden and unexpected loss, a betrayal, a time of doubt—you can recall that you are not like a willow tree with shallow roots, susceptible to every passing storm. You—by God's work—are like an elm or oak with a massive root system that goes deep and holds fast. The healthy life of faith is both about the foliage and fruit at the top and the strength and health in the roots.

When something happens that tears us down, we have the assurance that we have been "rooted and built up" and "strengthened" in Christ. We didn't build the superstructure of faith. It is God's truth, and we live in the shelter of it.

All of this leads to thanksgiving, and that, too, keeps us walking in the right direction. When we have a strong sense of gratitude for what God has meant and what God has done in the tough times and in the easy times, the act of thanksgiving keeps us looking up. Many of the psalms say, "I lift up my eyes," (Ps. 121:1; 123:1) because that is when we can see God ahead of us. Carrying a chip on your shoulder because you think God hasn't done enough lately undercuts any effort to get closer to God or be strengthened by him.

That brings us to a second point mentioned in this passage from Colossians: the challenge of "hollow philosophies" that can have a captivating allure but that are essentially deceptions. Dealing with doubt is sometimes a matter of dismay and discouragement because of life's difficulties, but sometimes doubt is the wreckage resulting from deception.

The phenomenally bestselling novel *The Da Vinci Code* by Dan Brown presented a very new and very old non-gospel (by that I mean that there is very little good news in Brown's story). The fiction is clearly in the foreground, as is the case with all novels, but the historical background about who Jesus really was and is takes the twisted shape of conspiracy and cover-up. The Lord of heaven and Earth is demoted to the level of a good man, a husband and father, who produced a progeny but no legacy. One of the strangest things about Dan Brown's story is that it makes Jesus a mere mortal and then doesn't even bother to make him a notable mortal. In the film version, the edge is taken off—maybe it's okay to pray to this Jesus (it can't really do any harm), but that's up to you. "The only thing that matters is what you believe," says one of the film's characters.

But something else really riveted my attention when I read the novel. The last paragraphs of *The Da Vinci Code* have the main character, Robert Langdon, standing at the place where the bones of Mary Magdalene (in the story) may be found:

> Like the murmurs of spirits in the darkness, forgotten words echoed. The quest of the Holy Grail is the quest to kneel before the bones of Mary Magdalene. . . . With a sudden upwelling of reverence, Robert Langdon fell to his knees. For a moment, he thought he heard a woman's voice . . . the wisdom of the ages . . . whispering up from the chasms of the earth.

The implication of these climactic lines is that something good for our lives can come from "murmurs of spirits in the darkness" and "whispering up from the chasms of the earth." I wonder how many people really want to believe that conclusion.

If we're living in an age of faith, we are also living in an age of doubt. Sometimes doubt arises because of personal crisis (that's just one kind of situation), but sometimes doubt takes hold because the philosophies of human invention and spiritual deception are setting the agenda of the day. In that case, it all gets mixed up with who has the right to say what, and people think that Christians are just too uptight, not open-minded enough, and want to be too controlling.

Here, briefly, is the story of the search for faith since the coming of Jesus. The first-century world into which Jesus came offered a potpourri of religions and philosophies. Rather like today, the Greco-Roman world had a religion on every corner and a philosopher's school on every street. In that dynamic mix, the message of who Jesus is, what he accomplished, and what he offers spread like nothing before. A whole civilization developed out of that faith; but along the way, the Church, at different times, misrepresented Jesus and was an all-too-human institution. That brings us to the modern era, when in the 1700s and 1800s people turned to reason as a better alternative than religion. Science became the way to true knowledge—the only source of knowledge, really. But as the war-torn decades of the twentieth century unfolded, a lot of people found that "modernism" cold and without meaning. You can't get a purpose for life out of a test tube. And with this "postmodern" mindset, people have said, "Maybe we should go looking for God again; maybe supernatural things have happened; maybe Jesus is important. Let's go looking."

The Gnostic movement of the third and fourth centuries tried to reinterpret Jesus, but it became an opportunity for people to be curious and to look back to the first century at the first beliefs of the early Christians.

Colossians 2:9-12 says:

For in Christ all the fullness of the Deity lives in bodily form, and you have been given fullness in Christ, who is the head over every power and authority. In him you were also circumcised, in the putting off of the sinful nature, not with a circumcision done by the hands of men but with the circumcision done by Christ, having been buried with him in baptism and raised with him through your faith in the power of God, who raised him from the dead.

What is "the fullness of deity in Jesus"? And how can it be? Is it a mystery? Absolutely. Is it beyond our comprehension? Yes. But this is exactly what you'd expect from a good God.

The best news of all is this: human beings have been offered "fullness" in Christ. Not the fullness of deity; God remains God and we remain human. Human is not divine any more than a pot is the same as the potter or the painting is the same as the painter. But the Christian gospel—the really good news of the day—says this: in

Christ, you can have the fullness of everything you really need. It all begins with God forgiving you for your faults and shortcomings and sins. This is not an easy forgiveness. For our sakes, the innocent Son of God went through humiliation and suffering and a death He should not have been subject to. And so He says to us: To be forgiven, you have to go through a kind of death yourself. Baptism is a picture of this burial of the old self so that a new self can emerge. And if you die to yourself—in the sense of giving up your personal prerogatives, your arbitrary and imaginative ideas of who God is—then you will surely be raised by the power of God to live a new life.

(Excerpt from *I Want to Believe* by Mel Lawrenz, copyright © 2007. Used by permission of Baker Books, a division of Baker Publishing Group.)

* * *

Can the year ahead be better than the last? Yes, certainly. But every passing year is a mix of blessing and struggle. We will all face some things in the year ahead that we just have to cope with, and other problems that we can solve. With God's help, we will move ahead.

We close with a few prayers: for us, for our communities, our nation, and our world. And key prayers from the Scriptures.

PRAYER

A Prayer of Faith

(audio version at www.wordway.org/audioprayers)

O God,

I now know that I want my life to be fully in your hands. This is right. It is time for me to hold back no longer.

You have brought me to this place. I know I am not merely imagining that you are real, and I am not just following what my friends and family want.

And so I confess to you that I am a sinner. I have sinned in my thoughts, and in my words, and in my deeds. Sometimes I sinned intentionally, and often-times by mistake. I want you to be the master of my life, not sin.

I confess that I believe in Jesus Christ. Though I have much to learn, I understand Jesus came to save us from our sins. His life was perfect, and in his death on the cross he offered forgiveness. He is Lord of all.

I humbly accept your great gift of mercy. You have done this, great God.

Heavenly Father, I want to live under your care every day.

Lord Jesus, it is right for me to follow you.

Holy Spirit, I am empty unless you fill me, broken unless you heal me, weak unless you empower me.

I am uncertain of what will happen next in my life, so help me, dear God, to have faith every day. Bring people into my life who can teach me what life in Jesus can be. I throw myself on your mercy today.

I pray this prayer with faith in you and in your amazing grace.

Amen.

(from *Prayers for Our Lives: 95 Lifelines to God for Everyday Circumstances* by Mel Lawrenz)

PRAYER

For the Community

Dear God,
We pray for our community.
We begin by thanking you for your rich blessings. We thank you for the care and purpose with which you created the heavens and the earth. Thank you that we can see the splendor of your creation. We see the majesty of your character in what you have made: the streams and hills, the lakes and forests, in fields that bear rich harvests.

We thank you for your influence in our culture and heritage. Help us to cling to values that stretch well beyond ourselves and the brief time we spend in this world.

We confess to you that our response to your goodness is often muted because we get entangled in things that are temporary and passing away.

We ask for your forgiveness and your mercy, and ask that you would drive us to faith and direct our vision to building our lives and communities with truth and integrity.

We pray now that you would help every person who has a role in governing our community and nation to understand the value you place on what they do. Help each one to sense the satisfaction that comes from being a public servant.

We pray specifically for matters of great weight that must be dealt with in these days: matters of public security and of social justice and of fiscal management. As the Bible invites us to ask you for wisdom whenever we need it—we do ask on behalf of every person making decisions that affect the lives of many, that you would give a wisdom that is deep and selfless and true.

We thank you that you hear our prayers, and long to hear prayers both made in public and voiced in the quiet corners of our lives. And so we pray for your providential care and protection over our community.

Amen.

(from *Prayers for Our Lives: 95 Lifelines to God for Everyday Circumstances* by Mel Lawrenz)

PRAYER

For the Nation

(audio version at www.wordway.org/audioprayers)

Dear God,

You have blessed us with the gift of life, and so, with every breath we take, we are your testimony of the value and sanctity of life. You have blessed us by putting us in a world that is your spectacular creation full of wonder; and you allow us to live in a nation rich with natural resources and incredible beauty. Help us to marvel at the blessings of your creation and to be responsible stewards of the land you have made.

You have blessed us with marriage and family and friendship. And so we ask you to help us cherish and respect these relationships you have woven into the human race, and may we honor those relationships by living them out with grace and truth.

You have blessed us with the gift of freedom.

The freedom by which we can gather together.

The freedom by which we make sober choices about how we conduct ourselves as a nation.

The freedom by which we can show acts of mercy to those who suffer or are disadvantaged.

The freedom by which we as citizens may exercise responsible discernment in the selection of our leaders.

The freedom by which we as fathers and mothers, sisters and brothers, and friends and neighbors and fellow-workers can build each other up to be the people you created us to be.

We pray for the leaders of our nation. Please bless and empower and guide them in these days which are the stepping stones to our future.

We acknowledge our daily need for your forgiveness of our shortcomings, and acknowledge our need for your protection against those who would harm and destroy. We are citizens of this nation, but we know that, to you, all the nations are together like a drop in a bucket, as dust on the scales.

We are today and always under your watchful eye as loving Father, saving Son, and purifying Holy Spirit.

Amen.

(from *Prayers for Our Lives: 95 Lifelines to God for Everyday Circumstances* by Mel Lawrenz)

PRAYER

For the World

(audio version at www.wordway.org/audioprayers)

Do you not know?
Have you not heard?
Has it not been told you from the beginning?
Have you not understood since the earth was found-
ed?
He sits enthroned above the circle of the earth,
and its people are like grasshoppers.
He stretches out the heavens like a canopy,
and spreads them out like a tent to live in.
He brings princes to naught
and reduces the rulers of this world to nothing.
Isaiah 40:21-23

Great Lord of heaven and earth,
We pray for our world.
But it is not our world, of course, it is your world.
By your sovereign choice you created the heavens
and the earth. Your power and beauty are every-
where to be seen in the creation. You chose to make
humanity according to your image.

But we men and women have chosen to follow our own ways. We separated ourselves from you. We ruined the world.

We rejoice that you so loved the world, that you have come in the person of Jesus Christ to save us.

And so we pray for the process of salvation in our world.

Help us to see your light even when darkness seems to surround us.

Help us to proclaim Jesus Christ, the light that has come into the world, at every opportunity.

Grant freedom so we may proclaim the gospel without impediment.

Help those whose very lives are threatened in persecution.

Bring your holy judgment against all evil.

Let your justice roll on like a river.

Bring peace to troubled regions of the world.

Guide us into the ways we can be peacemakers, as the Lord Jesus commanded.

Give us the courage to be peacemakers when others only want conflict and war.

Build in us an integrity of attitude, behavior, and character that will let the world know that we can return to your goodness.

In the powerful name of Jesus, Amen.

A BETTER YEAR AHEAD?

(from *Prayers for Our Lives: 95 Lifelines to God for Everyday Circumstances* by Mel Lawrenz)

PRAYER FROM SCRIPTURE

The Lord's Prayer

Our Father in heaven,
hallowed be your name,
your kingdom come,
your will be done,
on earth as it is in heaven.
Give us today our daily bread.
And forgive us our debts,
as we also have forgiven our debtors.
And lead us not into temptation,
but deliver us from the evil one.

Matthew 6:9–13

PRAYER FROM SCRIPTURE

Prayer for the Abundant Life

And this is my prayer: that your love may abound more and more in knowledge and depth of insight, so that you may be able to discern what is best and may be pure and blameless for the day of Christ, filled with the fruit of righteousness that comes through Jesus Christ—to the glory and praise of God.

Philippians 1:9-11

PRAYER FROM SCRIPTURE

Longing for God

You, God, are my God,
earnestly I seek you;
    I thirst for you,
my whole being longs for you,
    in a dry and parched land
where there is no water.
    I have seen you in the sanctuary
and beheld your power and your glory.
    Because your love is better than life,
my lips will glorify you.
    I will praise you as long as I live,
and in your name I will lift up my hands.
    I will be fully satisfied as with the richest of foods;
with singing lips my mouth will praise you.

Psalm 63:1-5

PRAYER FROM SCRIPTURE

Prayer of Confession

Have mercy on me, O God,
according to your unfailing love;
   according to your great compassion
blot out my transgressions.
   Wash away all my iniquity
and cleanse me from my sin.
   For I know my transgressions,
and my sin is always before me.
   Cleanse me with hyssop, and I will be clean;
wash me, and I will be whiter than snow.
   Let me hear joy and gladness;
let the bones you have crushed rejoice.
   Hide your face from my sins
and blot out all my iniquity.
   Create in me a pure heart, O God,
and renew a steadfast spirit within me.
   Do not cast me from your presence
or take your Holy Spirit from me.
   Restore to me the joy of your salvation
and grant me a willing spirit, to sustain me.

Psalm 51:1-3, 7-12

PRAYER FROM SCRIPTURE

Prayer for Strength, Love, and the Fullness of God

For this reason I kneel before the Father, from whom every family in heaven and on earth derives its name. I pray that out of his glorious riches he may strengthen you with power through his Spirit in your inner being, so that Christ may dwell in your hearts through faith. And I pray that you, being rooted and established in love, may have power, together with all the Lord's holy people, to grasp how wide and long and high and deep is the love of Christ, and to know this love that surpasses knowledge—that you may be filled to the measure of all the fullness of God.

Now to him who is able to do immeasurably more than all we ask or imagine, according to his power that is at work within us, to him be glory in the church and in Christ Jesus throughout all generations, for ever and ever! Amen.

Ephesians 3:14–21

For more resources, including downloadable group guides...

www.WordWay.org

Made in the USA
Monee, IL
30 November 2020